In the Year 1940

by

Kerry Butters.

In the Year 1940.

Millennium:	**2nd millennium**
Centuries:	19th century – **20th century** – 21st century
Decades:	1910s 1920s 1930s – **1940s** – 1950s 1960s 1970s
Years:	1937 1938 1939 – **1940** – 1941 1942 1943

1940 (MCMXL) was a leap year starting on Monday (dominical letter GF) of the Gregorian calendar, the 1940th year of the Common Era (CE) and *Anno Domini* (AD) designations, the 940th year of the 2nd millennium, the 40th year of the 20th century, and the 1st year of the 1940s decade.

Contents

Events

January

- January 4 – WWII: Axis powers: Luftwaffe General Hermann Göring assumes control of most war industries in Germany.
- January 6 – WWII: Winter War: General Semyon Timoshenko takes command of all Soviet forces.
- January 8
    - WWII: Winter War – Battle of Suomussalmi: The Soviet 44th Rifle Division is destroyed by Finnish forces.
    - WWII: Food rationing begins in Great Britain.
- January 9 – WWII; British submarine HMS *Starfish* is sunk.
- January 10 – WWII: Mechelen incident: A German plane carrying secret plans for the invasion of western Europe makes a forced landing in Belgium, leading to mobilization of defense forces in the Low Countries.
- January 19 – The Three Stooges short subject comedy film *You Nazty Spy!* released, the first Hollywood parody of Adolf Hitler and the Nazis, with Moe Howard portraying "Moe Hailstone" as the Hitler-parody lead.
- January 26 – Brisbane, Australia swelters through its hottest day ever, 43.2 degrees Celsius (109.76 Fahrenheit).
- January 27 – WWII: A peace resolution introduced in the Parliament of South Africa is defeated 81–59.
- January 29 – Three gasoline-powered trains carrying factory workers crash and explode while approaching Ajikawaguchi

Station, Yumesaki Line (Nishinari Line), Osaka, Japan, killing at least 181 people and injuring at least 92.

February

- February 1 – WWII: Winter War – Soviet forces launch a major assault on Finnish troops occupying the Karelian Isthmus.
- February 2 – Vsevolod Meyerhold is executed in the Soviet Union on charges of treason and espionage. He is cleared of all charges 15 years later in the first waves of de-Stalinization
- February 7 – RKO release Walt Disney's second full-length animated film, *Pinocchio*.
- February 9 – Mae West & W. C. Fields join comedic forces for *My Little Chickadee* with tremendous success. The film becomes one of the highest grossing of the year.
- February 10 – Tom and Jerry make their debut in *Puss Gets the Boot*. However it is not until 1941 that their current names are adopted.
- February 16 – WWII: *Altmark* Incident: The British destroyer HMS *Cossack* pursues the German tanker *Altmark* into the neutral waters of Jøssingfjord in southwestern Norway and frees the 290 British seamen held aboard.
- February 22 – In Tibet, province of Ando, 4-year-old Tenzin Gyatso is proclaimed the *tulku* (rebirth) of the thirteenth Dalai Lama.
- February 27 – Martin Kamen and Sam Ruben discover carbon-14.
- February 29 – Hattie McDaniel becomes the first African-American to win an Academy Award.

March

- March 2 – Cartoon character Elmer Fudd makes his debut in the animated short *Elmer's Candid Camera*.
- March 3 – In Sweden, a time bomb destroys the office of *Norrskenflamman* (a Swedish communist newspaper), killing 5.

- March 5 – Katyn massacre: Members of the Soviet Politburo (Joseph Stalin, Vyacheslav Molotov, Lazar Kaganovich, Mikhail Kalinin, Kliment Voroshilov and Lavrentiy Beria) sign an order, prepared by Beria, for the execution of 25,700 Polish intelligentsia, including 14,700 Polish POWs.
- March 11 – Ed Ricketts, John Steinbeck and six others leave Monterey, California for the Gulf of California on a collecting expedition.
- March 12 – The Soviet Union and Finland sign a peace treaty in Moscow ending the Winter War; Finns, along with the world at large, are shocked by the harsh terms.
- March 18 – WWII: Axis powers: Adolf Hitler and Benito Mussolini meet at Brenner Pass in the Alps. After being informed by Hitler that the Germans are ready to attack in the west, Mussolini agrees to bring Italy into the war in due course.
- March 21 – Édouard Daladier resigns as prime minister of France; Paul Reynaud succeeds him.
- March 23
  - Pakistan Movement: The Lahore Resolution, calling for greater autonomy for what will become Pakistan in British India, is drawn up by the All-India Muslim League during a three-day general session at Iqbal Park, Lahore.
  - *Truth or Consequences* debuts on NBC Radio.
- March 31 – WWII: Commerce raiding German auxiliary cruiser *Atlantis*, leaves the Wadden Sea for what will become the longest warship cruise of the war. (622 days without in-port replenishment or repair)

April

- April – Robin the Boy Wonder, Batman's trusted sidekick, makes his debut in *Detective Comics* #38.
- April 3 – WWII: Operation *Weserübung*: German ships set out for the invasion of Norway.

- April 4 – Neville Chamberlain, Prime Minister of the United Kingdom, in what proves to be a tragic misjudgment, declares in a major public speech that Hitler has "missed the bus".
- April 7 – Booker T. Washington becomes the first African American to be depicted on a United States postage stamp.
- April 8 – WWII: Operation Wilfred: The British fleet lays naval mines off the coast of neutral Norway.
- April 9 – WWII: Germany invades the neutral countries of Denmark and Norway in Operation *Weserübung*, opening the Norwegian Campaign. The British Royal Navy attempts to attack elements of the German fleet off Norway. Vidkun Quisling proclaims a new collaborationist regime in Norway. The German invasion of Denmark lasts for about six hours before that country capitulates.
- April 10 – WWII: First Naval Battle of Narvik: The British Royal Navy attacks the German fleet in the Ofotfjord. At Bergen, German cruiser *Königsberg* is sunk by British Fleet Air Arm Blackburn Skua dive bombers flying from RNAS Hatston in Orkney.
- April 12
  - The Faroe Islands are occupied by British troops, following the German invasion of Denmark. This action is taken to avert a possible German occupation of the islands with serious consequences for the course of the Battle of the Atlantic.
  - Opening day at Jamaica Race Course features the use of parimutuel betting equipment, a departure from bookmaking heretofore used exclusively throughout New York. Other tracks in the state follow suit later in 1940.
- April 13
  - WWII: Second Naval Battle of Narvik: The British Royal Navy causes all eight defending German destroyers in the Ofotfjord to be sunk.

- o The New York Rangers win the 1940 Stanley Cup Finals in ice hockey. It will be another 54 years before their next win in 1994.
- April 14 – Norwegian Campaign: First British ground forces land in Norway at Namsos and Harstad.
- April 16 – The Cleveland Indians, behind Bob Feller's Opening Day no-hitter, defeat the Chicago White Sox, 1-0.
- April 21 – *Take It or Leave It* makes its debut on CBS Radio, with Bob Hawk as host.
- April 23 – The Rhythm Club fire at a dance hall in Natchez, Mississippi, kills 198.

May

- May 6 – The International Olympic Committee formally cancels the 1940 Summer Olympics.
- May 10 – WWII:
  - o Battle of France begins
  - o German forces invade Low Countries
    - Battle of the Netherlands begins
    - Battle of Belgium begins
    - Invasion of Luxembourg begins
  - o British Invasion of Iceland.
  - o With the resignation of Neville Chamberlain, Winston Churchill becomes Prime Minister of the United Kingdom.

May 10: Winston Churchill

- May 13 – WWII:
  - Winston Churchill, in his first address as Prime Minister, tells the House of Commons of the United Kingdom, "I have nothing to offer you but blood, toil, tears, and sweat."
  - German armies open a 60-mile (97 km) wide breach in the Maginot Line at Sedan, France.
- May 13–May 14 – Queen Wilhelmina of the Netherlands and her government are evacuated to London using the British destroyer HMS *Hereward*.
- May 14 – WWII:
  - Rotterdam is subjected to savage terror bombing by the Luftwaffe; 980 are killed, and 20,000 buildings destroyed. General Henri Winkelman announces surrender of the Dutch army (outside Zeeland) to German forces
  - Recruitment begins in Britain for a home defence force: the Local Defence Volunteers, later known as the Home Guard.
- May 15
  - WWII: The Dutch Army formally signs a surrender document.
  - The very first McDonald's restaurant opens in San Bernardino, California.

- Women's stockings made of nylon are first placed on sale across the United States. Almost five million pairs are bought on this day.
- May 16 – President of the United States Franklin D. Roosevelt, addressing a joint session of the U.S. Congress, asks for an extraordinary credit of approximately $900 million to finance construction of at least 50,000 airplanes per year.
- May 17 – WWII:
  - Brussels falls to German forces; the Belgian government flees to Ostend.
  - Zeeland is overrun by German forces, ending the Battle of the Netherlands and beginning full German occupation of the Netherlands (Noord-Beveland surrenders on May 18 and remaining Dutch troops are withdrawn from Zeelandic Flanders on May 19).
- May 18 – Marshal Philippe Pétain is named vice-premier of France.
- May 19 – General Maxime Weygand replaces Maurice Gamelin as commander-in-chief of all French forces.
- May 20
  - WWII: German forces (2nd Panzer division), under General Rudolf Veiel, reach Noyelles on the English Channel.
  - Holocaust: The Nazi concentration camp and extermination camp Auschwitz-Birkenau, the largest of the German concentration camps, opens in occupied Poland near the town of Oświęcim. From now until January 1945, around 1.1 million people will be killed here.
- May 22 – WWII: The Parliament of the United Kingdom passes the Emergency Powers (Defence) Act 1939, giving the government full control over all persons and property.
- May 24 – WWII: The Anglo-French Supreme War Council decides to withdraw all forces under its control from Norway.
- May 26
  - WWII: The Dunkirk evacuation of the British Expeditionary Force starts.

- First free flight of Igor Sikorsky's Vought-Sikorsky VS-300 helicopter.
- May 28 WWII:
  - King Leopold III of Belgium orders the Belgian forces to cease fighting, ending the 18-day Battle of Belgium. Leaders of the Belgian government on French territory declare Leopold deposed.
  - In the land battle of Narvik, German forces retire giving the Allies their first victory on land in the war; however, the British have already decided to evacuate Narvik.
  - Winston Churchill warns the House of Commons of the United Kingdom to "prepare itself for hard and heavy tidings."
- May 29 – The Vought XF4U-1, prototype of the F4U Corsair U.S. fighter later used in WWII, makes its first flight.

June

- June 3
  - WWII: Paris is bombed by the Luftwaffe for the first time.
  - The Holocaust: Franz Rademacher proposes the Madagascar Plan.
  - Weather Bureau transferred to the United States Department of Commerce.
- June 4 – WWII:
  - The Dunkirk evacuation ends – the British and French navies together with large numbers of civilian vessels from various nations complete evacuating 300,000 troops from Dunkirk in France to England.
  - Winston Churchill tells the House of Commons of the United Kingdom, "We shall not flag or fail. We shall fight on the beaches... on the landing grounds... in the fields and the streets.... We shall never surrender."
- June 7
  - Daisy Duck debuts in *Mr. Duck Steps Out*.

- King Haakon VII of Norway and his government are evacuated from Tromsø to London on HMS *Devonshire*.
- June 9 – WWII: The British Commandos are created.
- June 10
  - WWII: Italy declares war on France and the United Kingdom.
  - WWII: U.S. President Franklin D. Roosevelt denounces Italy's actions with his "Stab in the Back" speech during the graduation ceremonies of the University of Virginia.
  - WWII: Canada declares war on Italy.
  - WWII: The Norwegian Army surrenders to German forces.
  - WWII: The French government flees to Tours.
  - Jamaican political activist Marcus Garvey dies of a stroke in London.
- June 11 – WWII: The Western Desert Campaign opens with British forces crossing the Frontier Wire into Italian Libya.
- June 12 – WWII: 13,000 British and French troops surrender to Major-General Erwin Rommel's 7th Panzer Division at Saint-Valery-en-Caux.
- June 13 – WWII: Paris is declared an open city.
- June 14
  - WWII: The French government flees to Bordeaux and Paris falls under German occupation.
  - WWII: U.S. President Franklin D. Roosevelt signs the Naval Expansion Act into law, which aims to increase the United States Navy's tonnage by 11%.
  - WWII: A group of 728 Polish political prisoners from Tarnów become the first residents of the Auschwitz concentration camp.
- June 15
  - WWII: The Soviet Union occupies Lithuania.
  - WWII: Verdun falls to German forces.
- June 16
  - The Churchill war ministry in the United Kingdom offers a Franco-British Union to Paul Reynaud, Prime Minister of

France, in the hope of preventing France from agreeing to an armistice with Germany, but Reynaud resigns when his own cabinet refuses to accept it.
- The Sturgis Motorcycle Rally is held for the first time in Sturgis, South Dakota.
- June 17
  - WWII: Philippe Pétain becomes Prime Minister of France and immediately asks Germany for peace terms.
  - WWII: The Soviet Union occupies Estonia and Latvia.
  - WWII: Operation Ariel begins: Allied troops start to evacuate France, following Germany's takeover of Paris and most of the nation.
  - WWII: RMS *Lancastria*, serving as a troopship, is bombed and sunk by Luftwaffe Junkers Ju 88 aircraft while evacuating British troops and nationals from Saint-Nazaire in France with the loss of at least 4,000 lives, the largest single UK loss in any World War II event, immediate news of which is suppressed in the British press. Destroyer HMS *Beagle* (H30) rescues around 600.
- June 18
  - WWII: Winston Churchill tells the House of Commons of the United Kingdom: "The Battle of France is over. The Battle of Britain is about to begin."
  - WWII: Appeal of 18 June: General Charles de Gaulle, *de facto* leader of the Free French Forces, makes his first broadcast appeal over Radio Londres from London rallying French Resistance, calling on all French people to continue the fight against Nazi Germany: "France has lost a battle. But France has not lost the war".
- June 22 – WWII: Second Armistice at Compiègne: The French Third Republic and Nazi Germany sign an armistice ending the Battle of France in the Forest of Compiègne, in the same Compagnie Internationale des Wagons-Lits railroad car used by Marshal Ferdinand Foch to agree the Armistice with Germany in 1918. This divides France into a *Zone occupée* in the north and

west under the Military Administration in France (Nazi Germany) and a southern *Zone libre*, Vichy France.

- June 23 – WWII: German leader Adolf Hitler surveys newly defeated Paris in now occupied France.
- June 24
  - United States politics: The Republican Party begins its national convention in Philadelphia and nominates Wendell Willkie as its candidate for president.
  - WWII: Vichy France signs armistice terms with Italy.
- June 25 – WWII: After the defeat of France, Hitler plans for an invasion of Switzerland, known as Operation Tannenbaum
- June 28 – General Charles de Gaulle is officially recognized by Britain as the "Leader of all Free Frenchmen, wherever they may be."
- June 30
  - WWII: German forces land in Guernsey, marking the start of the 5-year Occupation of the Channel Islands.
  - Federal government of the United States reorganisation:
    - The Civil Aeronautics Administration is placed under the Department of Commerce.
    - The U.S. Food and Drug Administration (FDA) is placed under the Federal Security Agency.
    - The United States Fish and Wildlife Service is placed under the Department of the Interior.

July

- July 1 – The first Tacoma Narrows Bridge opens for business, built with an 8-foot (2.4 m) girder and 190 feet (58 m) above the water, as the third longest suspension bridge in the world.
- July 2 – WWII: British-owned SS *Arandora Star*, carrying civilian internees and POWs of Italian and German origin from Liverpool to Canada, is torpedoed and sunk by the German submarine *U-47* off northwest Ireland with the loss of around 865 lives.

- July 3 – WWII: Attack on Mers-el-Kébir: British naval units sink or seize ships of the French fleet anchored in the Algerian ports of Mers-el-Kebir and Oran to prevent them falling into German hands. The following day, Vichy France breaks off diplomatic relations with Britain.
- July 6
  - Opening of Story Bridge in Brisbane.
  - British submarine HMS *Shark* is sunk.
- July 10 – WWII: The Battle of Britain begins.
- July 11
  - WWII: British destroyer HMS *Escort* is torpedoed and sunk by an Italian submarine.
  - WWII: Vichy France begins with a constitutional law which only 80 members of the parliament vote against. Philippe Pétain becomes Prime Minister of France.
- July 14 – WWII: Winston Churchill, in a worldwide broadcast, proclaims the intention of Great Britain to fight alone against Germany whatever the outcome: "We shall seek no terms. We shall tolerate no parley. We may show mercy. We shall ask none."
- July 15 – U.S. politics: The Democratic Party begins its national convention in Chicago, and nominates Franklin D. Roosevelt for an unprecedented third term as president.
- July 19
  - WWII: Allied victory at the Battle of Cape Spada HMAS *Sydney* and five destroyers sink the Italian cruiser *Bartolomeo Colleoni*.
  - WWII: Adolf Hitler makes a peace appeal to Britain in an address to the Reichstag. Lord Halifax, the British foreign minister, flatly rejects peace terms in a broadcast reply on July 22.
- July 21 – After rigged parliamentary elections in the three occupied countries on July 14–15, the parliaments proclaim the Estonian, Latvian and Lithuanian Soviet Socialist Republics
- July 23 – Welles Declaration: United States Under Secretary of State Sumner Welles announces that the U.S. will not accord

diplomatic recognition to the Soviet Union's occupation of the Baltic states.

- July 25 – General Henri Guisan addresses the officer corps of the Swiss army at Rütli resolving to resist any invasion of the country.
- July 27 – Bugs Bunny makes his debut in the Oscar-nominated cartoon short, *A Wild Hare*. However, it is not until 1941 that his name is adopted.

August

- August 1 – WWII: British submarine HMS *Spearfish* is sunk in the English Channel by what is much later discovered to be a mine.
- August 3 – The Lithuanian SSR is annexed into the Soviet Union, followed by the Latvian SSR on August 5 and the Estonian SSR August 6, just seven weeks after their occupation.
- August 3–19 – WWII: Italian conquest of British Somaliland.
- August 4 – Gen. John J. Pershing, in a nationwide radio broadcast, urges all-out aid to Britain in order to defend the Americas, while Charles Lindbergh speaks to an isolationist rally at Soldier Field in Chicago.
- August 8 – WWII: Wilhelm Keitel signs the "Aufbau Ost" directive, which eventually leads to the invasion of the Soviet Union.
- August 10 – WWII: British armed merchant cruiser HMS *Transylvania* is torpedoed off Malin Head, Ireland, by German submarine *U-56*.
- August 13 – WWII: The *Adlertag* ("Eagle Day") strike on southern England occurs, starting the rapid escalation of the Battle of Britain air offensive of the Luftwaffe against RAF Fighter Command.
- August 15 – Italy, without having declared war on Greece, sinks the Greek boat *Elli* (Ελλη).
- August 18 – HRH The Prince Edward, Duke of Windsor, is installed as Governor of the Bahamas.
- August 20

- WWII: Winston Churchill pays tribute in the House of Commons of the United Kingdom to the Royal Air Force: "Never in the field of human conflict was so much owed by so many to so few."
  - Leon Trotsky is attacked with an ice axe in his Mexico home by NKVD agent Ramón Mercader.
- August 21 – Leon Trotsky dies of injuries sustained.
- August 24 – Howard Florey and a team including Ernst Chain and Norman Heatley at the Sir William Dunn School of Pathology, University of Oxford, publish their laboratory results showing the *in vivo* bactericidal action of penicillin. They have also purified the drug.
- August 26 – WWII: Chad is the first French colony to proclaim its support for the Allies.
- August 30 – Second Vienna Award: Germany and Italy compel Romania to cede half of Transylvania to Hungary.

September

- September – The U.S. Army 45th Infantry Division (previously a National Guard Division in Arizona, Colorado, New Mexico, and Oklahoma), is activated and ordered into federal service for 1 year, to engage in a training program in Ft. Sill and Louisiana, prior to serving in WWII.
- September 2 – WWII: An agreement between America and Great Britain is announced to the effect that 50 U.S. destroyers needed for escort work will be transferred to Great Britain. In return, America gains 99-year leases on British bases in the North Atlantic, West Indies and Bermuda.
- September 4 – WWII: In Berlin, Adolf Hitler declares in a speech that Nazi Germany will avenge all night air raids carried out by England.
- September 5 – WWII: Commerce raiding German auxiliary cruiser *Komet* enters the Pacific Ocean via the Bering Strait after crossing

the Arctic Ocean from the North Sea with the help of Soviet icebreakers *Lenin*, *Stalin*, and *Kaganovich*.

- September 7
  - Treaty of Craiova: Romania loses Southern Dobruja to Bulgaria.
  - WWII: The Blitz – Nazi Germany begins to rain bombs on London (the first of 57 consecutive nights of strategic bombing).
- September 9 – Treznea massacre: The Hungarian Army, supported by local Hungarians kill 93 Romanian civilians in Treznea, Sălaj, a village in Northern Transylvania, as part of attempts to ethnic cleansing.
- September 12
  - In Lascaux, France, 17,000-year-old cave paintings are discovered by a group of young Frenchmen hiking through Southern France. The paintings depict animals and date to the Stone Age.
  - The Hercules Munitions Plant in Succasunna-Kenvil, New Jersey explodes, killing 55 people.
- September 14 – Ip massacre: The Hungarian Army, supported by local Hungarians, kill 158 Romanian civilians in Ip, Sălaj, a village in Northern Transylvania, as part of attempts at ethnic cleansing.
- September 16 – WWII: The Selective Training and Service Act of 1940 is signed into law by Franklin D. Roosevelt, creating the first peacetime draft in U.S. history.
- September 17–18 – WWII: SS *City of Benares* is torpedoed by German submarine *U-48* in the Atlantic with the loss of 248 of the 406 on board, including child evacuees bound for Canada. This results in cancellation of the British Children's Overseas Reception Board's plan to relocate children overseas.
- September 22 – Japan enters French Indochina: an agreement is signed in which Japan promises to station no more than 6,000 troops there, and never have more than 25,000 transiting the colony. Rights were also given for three airfields.

- September 25 – Occupation of Norway by Nazi Germany: German *Reichskommissar* Josef Terboven appoints a provisional council of state from the pro-Nazi Nasjonal Samling party under Vidkun Quisling as a puppet government for Norway.
- September 26 – A group of Japanese officers in violation of an agreement signed four days earlier with French Indochina, take Đồng Đăng and Lam Sơn with 40 Franco-Vietnamese troops killed and around 1,000 deserting. The same day the United States imposes a total embargo on all scrap metal shipments to Japan.
- September 27 – WWII: Germany, Italy and Japan sign the Tripartite Pact.

October

- October 1 – The first section of the Pennsylvania Turnpike, the United States' first long-distance controlled-access highway, is opened.
- October 11 – Portuguese-born performer Carmen Miranda makes her American film debut in *Down Argentine Way* one of the first films produced to promote the Good Neighbor policy.
- October 14 – The Balham tube station disaster in London, England, occurs during the Nazi Luftwaffe air raids on Great Britain.
- October 15 – Charlie Chaplin releases his brilliant and controversial wartime satire *The Great Dictator*, nine months after the Stooges' *You Nazty Spy!*.
- October 16 – The draft registration of approximately 16 million men begins in the United States.
- October 18–19 – WWII: Thirty-two ships are sunk from Convoy SC 7 and Convoy HX 79 by the most effective "wolfpack" of the war including U-boat aces Kretschmer, Prien and Schepke.
- October 26–28 – WWII: RMS *Empress of Britain*, serving as a troopship under the British flag, is bombed, torpedoed and sunk off the Donegal coast with the loss of 45 lives. At 42,348 GRT she is the war's largest merchant ship loss.

- October 28 – WWII: Italian troops invade Greece, meeting strong resistance from Greek troops and civilians. This action signals the beginning of the Balkan Campaign.
- October 29 – The Selective Service System lottery is held in Washington, D.C..

November

- November – In Cambodia the Khmer Issarak is formed to overthrow the French Army within the nation.
- November 2–8 – WWII (Greco-Italian War): In the Battle of Elaia–Kalamas in Epirus outnumbered Greek forces repel the Italian Army.
- November 5 – United States presidential election, 1940: Democrat incumbent Franklin D. Roosevelt defeats Republican challenger Wendell Willkie and becomes the United States' first and only third-term president.
- November 6 – Agatha Christie's mystery novel *And Then There Were None* is published in book form in the United States.
- November 7 – In Tacoma, Washington, the 600-foot (180 m)-long center span of the Tacoma Narrows Bridge (known as Galloping Gertie) collapses.
- November 8 – WWII: MS *City of Rayville* is sunk by a naval mine, the first United States Merchant Marine loss of the war, off Cape Otway, Australia.
- November 9 – Joaquín Rodrigo's *Concierto de Aranjuez* premieres in Barcelona, Spain.
- November 10 – 1940 Vrancea earthquake: An earthquake in Romania kills 1,000.
- November 11
  - WWII: The Royal Navy launches the first aircraft carrier strike in history, on the Italian battleship fleet anchored at Taranto naval base.

- o WWII: German auxiliary cruiser *Atlantis* captures top secret British mail intended for British Far East Command from the SS *Automedon* and sends it to Japan.
  - o Armistice Day Blizzard: An unexpected blizzard kills 144 in the Midwestern United States.
- November 13 – Walt Disney's *Fantasia* is released. It is the first box office failure for Disney, though it eventually recoups its cost years later, and becomes one of the most highly regarded of Disney's films.
- November 14 – WWII: The city centre of Coventry, England is destroyed by 500 Luftwaffe bombers: 150,000 fire bombs, 503 tons of high explosives, and 130 parachute mines level 60,000 of the city's 75,000 buildings; 568 people are killed, during the Coventry Blitz.
- November 15 – Abbott and Costello make their film debut in *One Night in the Tropics*.
- November 16
  - o WWII: In response to Germany levelling Coventry 2 days before, the Royal Air Force begins to bomb Hamburg (by war's end, 50,000 Hamburg residents will have died from Allied attacks).
  - o An unexploded pipe bomb is found in the Consolidated Edison office building (only years later is the culprit, George Metesky, apprehended).
  - o The Jamaica Association of Local Government Officers is founded.
- November 18 – WWII: German leader Adolf Hitler and Italian Foreign Minister Galeazzo Ciano meet to discuss Benito Mussolini's disastrous invasion of Greece.
- November 20 – WWII: Hungary, Romania and Slovakia join the Axis powers.
- November 25
  - o *Patria* disaster: As British authorities attempt to deport Jewish refugees (originating from German-occupied Europe) from Mandatory Palestine to Mauritius aboard the

requisitioned emigrant liner SS *Patria* at Haifa, the Jewish paramilitary organization Haganah sinks the ship with a bomb, killing around 250 refugees and crew.

- o de Havilland Mosquito and Martin B-26 Marauder military aircraft both make their first flights.
- o Woody Woodpecker makes his debut in the animated short *Knock Knock*.
- November 26–27 – Jilava Massacre: In Romania, coup leader General Ion Antonescu's Iron Guard arrests and executes over 60 of exiled king Carol II of Romania's aides, starting at a penitentiary near Bucharest. Among the dead is former minister and acclaimed historian Nicolae Iorga.
- November 27 – WWII: The British Royal Navy and Italian Regia Marina fight the Battle of Cape Spartivento.

December

- December – Timely Comics' Captain America Comics #1 (cover dated March 1941), first appearance of Captain America and Bucky, hits newsstands in the United States.
- December 1 – Manuel Ávila Camacho takes office as President of Mexico.
- December 6 – British submarine HMS *Regulus* is sunk near Taranto.
- December 8 – The Chicago Bears, in what will become the most one-sided victory in National Football League history, defeat the Washington Redskins 73–0 in the 1940 NFL Championship Game.
- December 9 – WWII: Operation Compass – British forces in North Africa begin their first major offensive with an attack on Italian forces at Sidi Barrani, Egypt.
- December 12 and December 15 – WWII: "Sheffield Blitz" ("Operation Crucible") – The Yorkshire city of Sheffield is badly damaged by German air-raids.
- December 14

- WWII British destroyers HMS *Hereward* and HMS *Hyperion* sink an Italian submarine off Bardia.
- Royal Navy Fairey Swordfish based on Malta bomb Tripoli.
- Plutonium is first synthesized in the laboratory by a team led by Glenn T. Seaborg and Edwin McMillan at the University of California, Berkeley.
- December 16 – WWII: Operation Abigail Rachel – RAF bombing of Mannheim.
- December 17 – President Roosevelt, at his regular press conference, first sets forth the outline of his plan to send aid to Great Britain that will become known as Lend-Lease.
- December 23 – WWII: Winston Churchill, in a broadcast address to the people of Italy, blames Benito Mussolini for leading his nation to war against the British, contrary to Italy's historic friendship with them: "One man has arrayed the trustees and inheritors of ancient Rome upon the side of the ferocious pagan barbarians."
- December 24 – Mahatma Gandhi, Indian spiritual non-violence leader writes his second letter to Adolf Hitler addressing him "My friend", requesting him to stop the war Germany had begun.
- December 29
  - Franklin D. Roosevelt, in a fireside chat to the nation, declares that the United States must become "the great arsenal of democracy."
  - WWII: "Second Great Fire of London" – Luftwaffe carries out a massive incendiary bombing raid, starting 1,500 fires. Many famous buildings, including the Guildhall and Trinity House, are either damaged or destroyed.
- December 30
  - California's first modern freeway, the future State Route 110, opens to traffic in Pasadena, California, as the Arroyo Seco Parkway (now the Pasadena Freeway).
  - In Sweden, Victor Hasselblad forms the Victor Hasselblad AB Camera Company.

Undated

- In Korea, the *Hunminjeongeum* (1446) is discovered, explaining the basis of the Hangul alphabet.
- US historian Arthur Marder publishes *The Anatomy of British Sea Power: a history of British naval policy in the pre-Dreadnought era, 1880-1905*.
- Walter Knott begins construction of ghost town replica which would soon evolve into Knott's Berry Farm.
- The plane Mitsubishi A6M Zero was designed, so named as 1940 roughly corresponds to the year 2600 on the Japanese Imperial calendar.

Births

January

Brian Josephson

Joachim Gauck

James Cromwell

- January 2 – Jim Bakker, American televangelist and former husband of Tammy Faye
- January 3 – Leo de Berardinis, Italian stage actor and theatre director (d. 2008)
- January 4
    - Brian Josephson, Welsh physicist, Nobel Prize laureate
    - Gao Xingjian, Chinese-born writer, Nobel Prize laureate
- January 6 – Penny Lernoux, American journalist and author (d. 1989)
- January 9 – Miguel Ángel Rodríguez, Costa Rican politician, lawyer, economist, and businessman
- January 14 – Julian Bond, American civil rights activist (d. 2015)
- January 16 – Franz Müntefering, German politician
- January 17
    - Tabaré Vázquez, President of Uruguay
    - Nerses Bedros XIX Tarmouni, Armenian Catholic Patriarch of Cilicia (d. 2015)
- January 19 – Mike Reid, English actor (d. 2007)
- January 20 – Carol Heiss, American figure skater
- January 21
    - Jeremy Jacobs, American businessman, owner (Boston Bruins)
    - Jack Nicklaus, American golfer
- January 22 – John Hurt, English actor
- January 24 – Joachim Gauck, German president

- January 27 – James Cromwell, American actor
- January 28 – Carlos Slim, Mexican businessman

February

H. R. Giger

George A. Romero

Peter Fonda

- February 1 – Ajmer Singh, Indian athlete and educator (d. 2010)
- February 2 – David Jason, English actor

- February 3 – Fran Tarkenton, American football player
- February 4 – George A. Romero, American film writer and director
- February 5 – H. R. Giger, Swiss artist (d. 2014)
- February 6
  - Tom Brokaw, American television news reporter
  - Jimmy Tarbuck, English comedian
- February 8 – Ted Koppel, American journalist
- February 9
  - Brian Bennett, British drummer and songwriter (The Shadows)
  - J. M. Coetzee, South African writer, Nobel Prize laureate
  - Seamus Deane, Irish poet and novelist
- February 12
  - Ralph Bates, English actor (d. 1991)
  - Richard Lynch, American actor (d. 2012)
- February 17 – Gene Pitney, American singer (d. 2006)
- February 18 – Fabrizio De André, Italian singer-songwriter (d. 1999)
- February 19 – Smokey Robinson, American musician
- February 20 – Jimmy Greaves, English footballer
- February 21 – Akihiko Kumashiro, Japanese politician
- February 22
  - Judy Cornwell, English actress
  - Johnson Mlambo, South African politician
  - Billy Name, American photographer and Warhol archivist
- February 23 – Peter Fonda, American actor
- February 24
  - Pete Duel, American actor (d. 1971)
  - Denis Law, Scottish football player
- February 25 – Ron Santo, American baseball player (d. 2010)
- February 27 – Howard Hesseman, American actor
- February 28
  - Mario Andretti, American race car driver
  - Joe South, American singer and songwriter (d. 2012)

March

Raúl Juliá

Chuck Norris

James Caan

Nancy Pelosi

- March 1 – Nuala O'Faolain, Irish journalist and author (d. 2008)
- March 3
  - Germán Castro Caycedo, Colombian writer and journalist
  - Owen Spencer-Thomas, English broadcaster, journalist and clergyman
- March 6 – Willie Stargell, American baseball player (d. 2001)
- March 7 – Rudi Dutschke, German radical student leader (d. 1979)
- March 8 – Susan Clark, Canadian actress (*Webster*)
- March 9 – Raúl Juliá, Puerto Rican actor (d. 1994)
- March 10
  - Chuck Norris, American actor and martial artist
  - Dean Torrence, American singer (Jan and Dean)
- March 12 – Al Jarreau, American singer
- March 13 – Candi Staton, American singer
- March 15 – Phil Lesh, American musician (Grateful Dead)
- March 16
  - Bernardo Bertolucci, Italian writer and film director
  - Jan Pronk, Dutch politician and diplomat
  - James Wong, Hong Kong composer (d. 2004)
- March 17 – Mark White, Governor of Texas
- March 21 – Solomon Burke, American singer and songwriter (d. 2010)
- March 22 – Haing S. Ngor, Cambodian actor (d. 1996)
- March 25
  - Anita Bryant, American entertainer
  - Mina, Italian singer
- March 26
  - James Caan, American actor
  - Nancy Pelosi, Speaker of the United States House of Representatives
- March 29
  - Ray Davis, American musician (P-Funk) (d. 2005)
  - Astrud Gilberto, Brazilian-born singer

April

Margrethe II of Denmark

Al Pacino

- April 1 – Wangari Maathai, Kenyan environmentalist, recipient of the Nobel Peace Prize (d .2011)
- April 2 – Penelope Keith, English actress
- April 8 – John Havlicek, American basketball player
- April 12
  - John Hagee, American televangelist
  - Herbie Hancock, American musician
- April 13 – Max Mosley, British motorsport boss
- April 16 – Queen Margrethe II of Denmark
- April 18 – Joseph L. Goldstein, American scientist, recipient of the Nobel Prize in Physiology or Medicine
- April 24 – Sue Grafton, American novelist
- April 25
  - Al Pacino, American actor

- o Tristram Powell, English television director, film director, writer and producer
- April 26 – Giorgio Moroder, Italian film composer

May

- May 1 – Elsa Peretti, Italian jewelry designer
- May 2 – Jo Ann Pflug, American former actress and motivational speaker
- May 5 – Lance Henriksen, American actor and potter
- May 7
  - o Angela Carter, English author and editor (d. 1992)
  - o Jim Connors, American radio personality (d. 1987)
- May 8
  - o Peter Benchley, American author (d. 2006)
  - o Ricky Nelson, American singer (d. 1985)
  - o Toni Tennille, American singer
- May 9 – James L. Brooks, American film producer and writer
- May 11 – Juan Downey, Chilean-born video artist (d. 1993)
- May 13 – Bruce Chatwin, British author (d. 1989)
- May 14 – 'H'. Jones, British soldier (VC recipient) (d. 1982)
- May 15
  - o Lainie Kazan, American actress and singer
  - o Don Nelson, American basketball player and coach
- May 17
  - o Alan Kay, American computer scientist
  - o Reynato Puno, Filipino Supreme Court Chief Justice
- May 18 – Lenny Lipton, American inventor
- May 20
  - o Stan Mikita, Slovakian-born Canadian hockey player
  - o Sadaharu Oh, Japanese baseball player
- May 22 – Bernard Shaw, American journalist and television news reporter
- May 24 – Joseph Brodsky, Russian-born poet, Nobel Prize laureate (d. 1996)

- May 29 – Farooq Leghari, President of Pakistan (d. 2010)

June

Tom Jones

Nancy Sinatra

John Mahoney

- June 1 – René Auberjonois, American actor
- June 2 – Constantine II of Greece
- June 4 – Ludwig Schwarz, Austrian bishop
- June 6 – Richard Paul, American actor (d. 1998)
- June 7

- o Monica Evans, British actress
- o Tom Jones, Welsh singer
- June 8 – Nancy Sinatra, American singer
- June 16
  - o Carole Ann Ford, British actress
  - o Neil Goldschmidt, Governor of Oregon
  - o Taylor Gun-Jin Wang, Chinese-American astronaut
- June 17
  - o George Akerlof, American economist, Nobel Prize laureate
  - o Alan Murray, Australian professional golfer
- June 19 – Paul Shane, English-born actor (d. 2013)
- June 20 – John Mahoney, English-born actor
- June 21 – Mariette Hartley, American actress
- June 22
  - o Abbas Kiarostami, Iranian film director, screenwriter, and film producer
  - o Esther Rantzen, British broadcaster
- June 23
  - o Adam Faith, English singer and actor (d. 2003)
  - o Lord Irvine of Lairg, Lord Chancellor of England
  - o Wilma Rudolph, American athlete (d. 1994)
- June 25 – A. J. Quinnell, English writer (d. 2005)
- June 27 – Anil Karanjai, Indian painter of the Hungry generation movement.
- June 28 – Muhammad Yunus, founder of Grameen Bank, Nobel Prize laureate
- June 29 – Vyacheslav Artyomov, Russian composer

July

Ringo Starr

Sir Patrick Stewart

James Brolin

Roy Walker

- July 2 – Christopher Awdry, English children's writer & son of Wilbert Awdry
- July 3
  - César Tovar, Venezuelan baseball player
  - Fontella Bass, American soul singer (d. 2012)
- July 6 – Nursultan Abishuly Nazarbayev, President of Kazakhstan
- July 7 – Ringo Starr, British drummer (The Beatles)
- July 10
  - Gene Alley, American baseball player
  - Helen Donath, American soprano
  - Tom Farmer, Scottish entrepreneur
- July 13
  - Paul Prudhomme, American celebrity chef and cookbook author
  - Patrick Stewart, English actor
- July 17
  - Tim Brooke-Taylor, English comedian
  - Verne Lundquist, American sportscaster
- July 18
  - James Brolin, American actor and director
  - Joe Torre, American baseball player and manager
- July 22 – Alex Trebek, Canadian game show host
- July 24 – Stanley Hauerwas, American theologian
- July 26 – Mary Jo Kopechne, American aide to Ted Kennedy (d. 1969)

- July 27
  - Pina Bausch, German choreographer (d. 2009)
  - Bharati Mukherjee, Indian-born novelist
- July 31 – Roy Walker, Northern Irish comedian

August

Martin Sheen

Jack Thompson

- August 1 – Ram Loevy, Israeli screenwriter and director
- August 3 – Martin Sheen, American actor, father of Charlie Sheen
- August 7 – Jean-Luc Dehaene, Prime Minister of Belgium (d. 2014)
- August 8 – Dilip Sardesai, former Indian cricketer (d. 2007)
- August 10 – Bobby Hatfield, American singer (The Righteous Brothers) (d. 2003)
- August 13 – Dirk Sager, German journalist (d. 2014)
- August 14
  - Galen Hall, American football coach
  - Max Schautzer, Austrian born, German radio and television presenter

- August 19 – Jill St. John, American actress
- August 20
    - Musa Geshaev, Chechen poet and historian (d. 2014)
    - Rubén Hinojosa, American politician
- August 23 – Tom Baker, American actor (d. 1982)
- August 25 – José van Dam, Belgian bass-baritone
- August 27
    - Fernest Arceneaux, American musician (d. 2008)
    - Sonny Sharrock, American jazz musician (d. 1994)
- August 29
    - Bennie Maupin, American musician
    - Johnny Paris, American musician (Johnny and the Hurricanes) (d. 2006)
    - Wim Ruska, Dutch wrestler and martial artist (d. 2015)
- August 31
    - Wilton Felder, American saxophonist and bassist (d. 2015)
    - Jack Thompson, Australian actor

September

Pauline Collins

Raquel Welch

Linda Gray

- September 3
  - Joseph C. Strasser, American admiral
  - Eduardo Galeano, Uruguayan writer (d. 2015)
  - Pauline Collins, English actress
- September 5 – Raquel Welch, American actress
- September 7
  - Abdurrahman Wahid, former President of Indonesia (d. 2009)
  - Dario Argento, Italian filmmaker.
- September 10 – David Mann, American artist (d. 2004)
- September 11
  - Brian De Palma, American film director
  - Ajit Singh, Indian-born economist (d. 2015)
- September 12
  - Linda Gray, American model and actress
  - Skip Hinnant, American actor
  - Mickey Lolich, American baseball player
- September 13 – Óscar Arias, Costa Rican politician, recipient of the Nobel Peace Prize
- September 14 – Larry Brown, American basketball coach
- September 18 – Frankie Avalon, American singer and actor
- September 20 – Tarō Asō, 59th Prime Minister of Japan
- September 23 – Mohammad-Reza Shajarian, Iranian traditional singer
- September 24 – Michiko Suganuma, Urushi Japanese lacquer artist

October

John Lennon

Michael Gambon

Pelé

- October 9 – John Lennon, British musician and singer (The Beatles) (d. 1980)
- October 13 – Pharoah Sanders, American saxophonist
- October 14 – Cliff Richard, American pop Sensation
- October 15 – Peter C. Doherty, Australian immunologist, recipient of the Nobel Prize in Physiology or Medicine
- October 16 – Ivan Della Mea, Italian singer-songwriter (d. 2009)
- October 19 – Sir Michael Gambon, Irish actor

- October 20 – Robert Pinsky, United States Poet Laureate
- October 21
  - Geoffrey Boycott, English cricketer
  - Manfred Mann, South African rock musician
- October 23 – Pelé, Brazilian footballer
- October 24 – Yossi Sarid, Israeli politician (d. 2015)
- October 25 – Bobby Knight, American basketball coach
- October 27 – John Gotti, American gangster (d. 2002)
- October 28 – Jack Shepherd, English actor

November

Bruce Lee

Qaboos bin Said al Said

- November 1 – Ramesh Chandra Lahoti, Chief Justice of India
- November 2 – Carolin Reiber, German television presenter
- November 11 – Turan Emeksiz, Turkish student killed in demonstrations (d. 1960)
- November 12 – Glenn Stetson, Canadian singer
- November 15

- ○ Roberto Cavalli, Italian designer
- ○ Sam Waterston, American actor
- November 17 – Luke Kelly, Irish ballad singer (The Dubliners)
- November 18 – Qaboos bin Said al Said, sultan of Oman
- November 20 – Helma Sanders-Brahms, German film director (d. 2014)
- November 21 – Richard Marcinko, U.S. Navy SEAL team member and author
- November 22
  - ○ Andrzej Żuławski, Polish film director and writer (d. 2016)
  - ○ Terry Gilliam, American-born British screenwriter, director and animator
- November 25
  - ○ Joe Gibbs, American football coach
  - ○ Percy Sledge, American singer (d. 2015)
- November 27 – Bruce Lee, Chinese-American martial artist and actor (d. 1973)
- November 29 – Chuck Mangione, American flugelhorn player

December

Richard Pryor

Frank Zappa

- December 1 – Richard Pryor, American actor and comedian (d. 2005)
- December 4
  - Freddy Cannon, American singer
  - Gary Gilmore, American murderer (d. 1977)
- December 5 – Peter Pohl, Swedish writer
- December 11 – Donna Mills, American actress and dancer
- December 12
  - Sharad Pawar, Indian politician
  - Dionne Warwick, American singer
- December 15
  - Barbara Valentin, Austrian actress (d. 2002)
- December 20 – Pat Chapman, English author
- December 21 – Frank Zappa, American musician, composer, and satirist (d. 1993)
- December 22 – Noel Jones, British ambassador to Kazakhstan (d. 1995)
- December 23
  - Jorma Kaukonen, American musician (Jefferson Airplane, Hot Tuna)
  - Robert Labine, former mayor of Gatineau, Quebec
- December 24 – Janet Carroll, American actress and singer (d. 2012)
- December 26 – Edward C. Prescott, American economist, Nobel Prize laureate

Date unknown

- Michael Jackson, New Zealand poet and anthropologist

Deaths

January

- January – Fusajiro Yamauchi, Japanese business executive (b. 1859)
- January 4 – Flora Finch, English-born actress and comedian (b. 1869)
- January 18 – Kazimierz Przerwa-Tetmajer, Polish poet and writer (b. 1865)
- January 27 – Isaac Babel, Ukrainian writer (executed) (b. 1894)

February

- February 1 – Philip Francis Nowlan, American science fiction writer, creator of *Buck Rogers* (b. 1888)
- February 2
    - Vsevolod Meyerhold, Russian theatre practitioner (b. 1874)
    - Mikhail Koltsov, Soviet journalist (executed) (b. 1898)
- February 4 – Samuel M. Vauclain, American engineer (b. 1856)
- February 9 – William Edward Dodd, American historian and diplomat (b. 1869)
- February 11 – John Buchan, 1st Baron Tweedsmuir, Scottish-born novelist and Governor General of Canada (b. 1875)
- February 26 – Michael Hainisch, 2nd President of Austria (b. 1858)
- February 27 – Peter Behrens, German architect and designer (b. 1868)
- February 29 – Edward Frederic Benson, English writer

March

Selma Lagerlöf

- March 1 – Anton Hansen Tammsaare, Estonian writer (b. 1878)
- March 5
  - Maxine Elliott, American actress (b. 1868)
  - Cai Yuanpei, Chinese educator (b. 1868)
- March 10 – Mikhail Bulgakov, Russian writer (b. 1891)
- March 11 – John Monk Saunders, American writer (b. 1897)
- March 16 – Selma Lagerlöf, Swedish writer, Nobel Prize laureate (b. 1858)
- March 20 – Alfred Ploetz, German physician, biologist, and eugenicist (b. 1860)
- March 26 – Spyridon Louis, Greek runner (b. 1873)
- March 27
  - Madeleine Astor, American survivor of the sinking of the RMS *Titanic* (b. 1893)
  - Michael Joseph Savage, Prime Minister of New Zealand (b. 1872)
- March 30 – George Egerton, British admiral (b. 1852)
- March 31 – Tinsley Lindley, English footballer (b. 1865)

April

Carl Bosch

- April 1 – John A. Hobson, English economist (b. 1858)
- April 21 – George Barnes, British Labour politician (b. 1859)
- April 26 – Carl Bosch, German chemist, Nobel Prize laureate (b. 1874)
- April 28 – Luisa Tetrazzini, Italian opera singer (b. 1871)

May

- May 7 – George Lansbury, British Labour politician (b. 1859)
- May 11 – Chujiro Hayashi, Japanese Reiki Master (b. 1880)
- May 14 – Emma Goldman, Lithuanian-born anarchist (b. 1869)
- May 15 – Menno ter Braak, Dutch writer (b. 1902)
- May 19 – Diego Mazquiarán, Spanish matador (b. 1895)
- May 20 – Verner von Heidenstam, Swedish writer, Nobel Prize laureate (b. 1859)
- May 25 – Joe De Grasse, Canadian film director (b. 1873)
- May 26 – Wilhelm of Prussia, Prussian prince (b. 1906)
- May 28
    - Prince Frederick Charles of Hesse (b. 1868)
    - Walter Connolly, American actor (b. 1887)
- May 29 – Mary Anderson, American stage actress (b. 1859)

June

Arthur Harden

Paul Klee

- June 7
  - James Hall, American actor (b. 1900)
  - Hugh Rodman, American admiral (b. 1859)
- June 10 – Marcus Garvey, Jamaican-born publisher, entrepreneur, and black nationalist (b. 1887)
- June 11 – Alfred S. Alschuler, American architect (b. 1876)
- June 13 – George Fitzmaurice, American director (b. 1885)
- June 14 – Henry W. Antheil, Jr., American diplomat (b. 1912)
- June 17 – Arthur Harden, English chemist, Nobel Prize laureate (b. 1865)
- June 19 – Maurice Jaubert, French composer (b. 1900)
- June 20 – Charley Chase, American comedian (b. 1893)
- June 21
  - Édouard Vuillard, French painter (b. 1868)
  - Smedley Butler, U.S. general (b. 1881)

- ○ Janusz Kusociński, Polish athlete (b. 1907)
- June 22 – Walter Hasenclever, German poet and playwright (b. 1890)
- June 28 – Italo Balbo, Italian Fascist leader (b. 1896)
- June 29 – Paul Klee, Swiss artist (b. 1879)

July

- July 1 – Ben Turpin, American actor (b. 1869)
- July 9– Józef Biniszkiewicz, Silesian politician (b. 1875)
- July 15 – Robert Wadlow, tallest man ever (infection) (b. 1918)
- July 30 – Spencer S. Wood, United States Navy rear admiral (b. 1861)

August

Leon Trotsky

Paul Nipkow

J. J. Thomson

- August 5 – Frederick Albert Cook, American explorer (b. 1865)
- August 8 – Johnny Dodds, American jazz clarinetist (b. 1892)
- August 13
  - James Fairbairn, Australian pastoralist, aviator, and politician (b. 1897)
  - Sir Henry Gullett, Australian politician (b. 1878)
  - Geoffrey Street, Australian politician (b. 1894)
  - Sir Brudenell White, Australian general (b. 1876)
- August 18 – Walter Chrysler, American automobile pioneer (b. 1875)
- August 21
  - Hermann Obrecht, Swiss Federal Councillor (b. 1882)
  - Leon Trotsky, Russian revolutionary (assassinated) (b. 1879)
- August 22
  - Sir Oliver Lodge, British physicist (b. 1851)
  - Gerald Strickland, 4th Prime Minister of Malta, 23rd Governor of New South Wales, 15th Governor of Western Australia and 9th Governor of Tasmania (b. 1861)
  - Mary Vaux Walcott, American artist and naturalist (b. 1860)
- August 24 – Paul Nipkow, German technician and inventor (b. 1860)
- August 28 – William Bowie, American geodetic engineer (b. 1872)
- August 30 – J. J. Thomson, English physicist, Nobel Prize laureate (b. 1856)

- August 31 – Ernest Lundeen, American lawyer and politician (b. 1878)

September

- September 4 – George William de Carteret, author from Jersey island (b. 1869)
- September 5 – Charles de Broqueville, former Prime Minister of Belgium (b. 1860)
- September 10 – Nikola Ivanov, Bulgarian general (b. 1861)
- September 23 – Hale Holden, president of Chicago, Burlington and Quincy Railroad 1914-1918 and 1920-1929 (b. 1869)
- September 25 – Marguerite Clark, American actress (b. 1883)
- September 26 – Walter Benjamin, German philosopher and cultural critic (b. 1892)
- September 27
  - Julius Wagner-Jauregg, Austrian neuroscientist, recipient of the Nobel Prize in Physiology or Medicine (b. 1857)
  - Julián Besteiro, Spanish socialist politician (b. 1870)

October

- October 5
  - Ballington Booth, American co-founder of Volunteers of America (b. 1857)
  - Lincoln Loy McCandless, Hawaiian politician and cattle rancher (b. 1859)
  - Silvestre Revueltas, Mexican composer (b. 1899)
- October 9 – Wilfred Grenfell, English medical missionary to Newfoundland and Labrador (b. 1865)
- October 10 – Berton Churchill, Canadian actor (b. 1876)
- October 11 – Adolf von Trotha, German admiral (b. 1868)
- October 12 – Tom Mix, American actor (b. 1880)
- October 15 – Lluís Companys, President of the Generalitat of Catalonia (executed) (b. 1882)

- October 17 – George Davis, American baseball player and MLB Hall of Famer (b. 1870)

November

Neville Chamberlain

- November 3 – Manuel Azaña, 2nd President of the Spanish Second Republic and 55th Prime Minister of Spain (b. 1880)
- November 5 – Otto Plath, father of American poet Sylvia Plath, and entomologist (b. 1885)
- November 9
  - Neville Chamberlain, former Prime Minister of the United Kingdom (b. 1869)
  - John Henry Kirby, Texas legislator and American businessman (b. 1860)
- November 17
  - Eric Gill, British sculptor and writer (b. 1882)
  - Raymond Pearl, American biologist (b. 1879)
- November 19 – Ralph W. Barnes, American journalist (b. 1899)
- November 27
  - Jean Chiappe, French civil servant (b. 1878)
  - Henri Guillaumet, French aviator (b. 1902)

December

F. Scott Fitzgerald

- December 2 – Nikolai Koltsov, Russian biologist and genetist (b. 1872)
- December 5 – Jan Kubelík, Czech violinist (b. 1880)
- December 14 – Anton Korošec, Slovenian political leader (b. 1872)
- December 15 or December 16 (unclear) – Billy Hamilton, American baseball player and MLB Hall of Famer (b. 1866)
- December 16 – Eugène Dubois, Dutch paleoanthropologist and geologist (b. 1858)
- December 19 – Kyösti Kallio, President of Finland (b. 1873)
- December 21 – F. Scott Fitzgerald, American writer (b. 1896)
- December 22 – Nathanael West, American writer (b. 1903)
- December 23 – Eddie August Schneider, American aviator (b. 1911)
- December 25 – Agnes Ayres, American actress (b. 1898)
- December 26 – Daniel Frohman, American theater producer (b. 1851)

Nobel Prizes

- Physics – not awarded
- Chemistry – not awarded
- Physiology or Medicine – not awarded
- Literature – not awarded
- Peace – not awarded

In the News.

Dunkirk nine day evacuation begins on May 27th of British Expeditionary Force.

Germany and Italy agree to form an alliance against France and the United Kingdom.

Britain Creates The Home Guard to act as the first line of defence in case of invasion.

Great Britain begins food rationing during World War II.

Germany starts it's Blitz on London on September 7th with 300 German bombers in the first of 57 consecutive nights of bombing.

Franklin D. Roosevelt wins the election and becomes the United States' first third-term president.

An annular solar eclipse is observed in the United States.

RMS Queen Elizabeth – enters into service.

Popular Films - Walt Disney's Pinocchio, The Great Dictator, starring Charlie Chaplin.

Nylon Stockings go on sale.

www.ingramcontent.com/pod-product-compliance
Lightning Source LLC
Chambersburg PA
CBHW071130280526
45787CB00003B/1230